SEP   2013

W9-BAJ-746

DISCARD

CPL discards materials that are outdated
and in poor condition
room for current   materials.
underused materials are offered for
public sale

LIGHTNING
BOLT
BOOKS™

Can You Tell a Velociraptor from a Deinonychus?

Buffy Silverman

Lerner Publications Company

Minneapolis

For Jake,
who sang about
Deinonychus many
years ago
—B.S.

Copyright © 2014 by Lerner Publishing Group, Inc.

All rights reserved. International copyright secured. No part of this book may be reproduced, stored in a retrieval system, or transmitted in any form or by any means — electronic, mechanical, photocopying, recording, or otherwise — without the prior written permission of Lerner Publishing Group, Inc., except for the inclusion of brief quotations in an acknowledged review.

Lerner Publications Company
A division of Lerner Publishing Group, Inc.
241 First Avenue North
Minneapolis, MN 55401 U.S.A.

Website address: www.lernerbooks.com

Library of Congress Cataloging-in-Publication Data

Silverman, Buffy.
    Can you tell a Velociraptor from a Deinonychus? / by Buffy Silverman.
        p.   cm. — (Lightning bolt books™—Dinosaur look-alikes)
    Includes index.
    ISBN 978-1-4677-1356-6 (library binding : alkaline paper)
    ISBN 978-1-4677-1760-1 (eBook)
    1. Velociraptor—Juvenile literature. 2. Deinonychus—Juvenile literature. 3. Dinosaurs—Juvenile literature. I. Title.
QE862.S3S4835 2014
567.912—dc23   2013005786

Manufactured in the United States of America
1 — BP — 7/15/13

Table of Contents

Small and Fierce

Imagine a dinosaur on the hunt. You may picture a giant taller than a building. But not all dinosaurs were big.

How big do you think this Deinonychus was?

Velociraptor and Deinonychus were small dinosaurs. They were shorter than your parents! But they were fierce predators. Predators hunt other animals.

Velociraptor was small but dangerous.

These dinos ran on two legs. Long, stiff tails helped them balance. They bit with strong jaws. Sharp teeth tore meat.

A tail balanced the weight of this dinosaur's head.

Raptor comes from a word that means "capture."

Velociraptor and Deinonychus were dinosaurs called raptors. Raptors had large hands with three big fingers. They used their hands to grab prey. Prey is an animal hunted for food.

Look at the raptors' feet. Each foot had one extra-large claw. The dinos raised this claw when they walked. The sharp claw was a weapon. It probably pinned down prey.

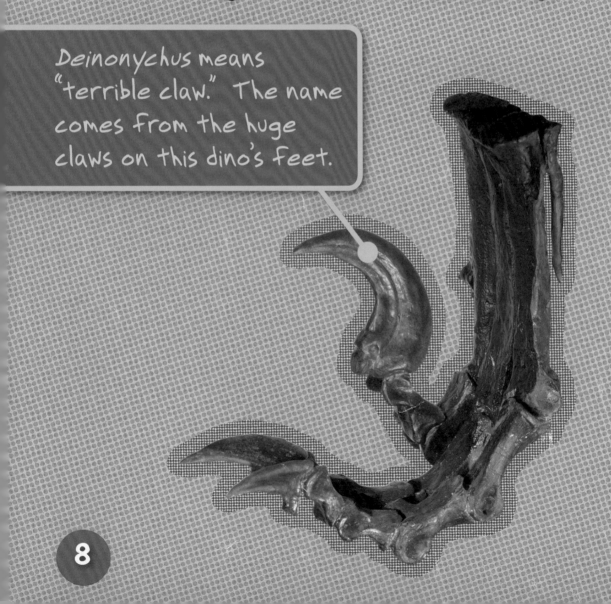

Deinonychus means "terrible claw." The name comes from the huge claws on this dino's feet.

You can tell these hunters apart. **Deinonychus was larger than Velociraptor.** It was 3 to 4 feet (about 1 meter) tall.

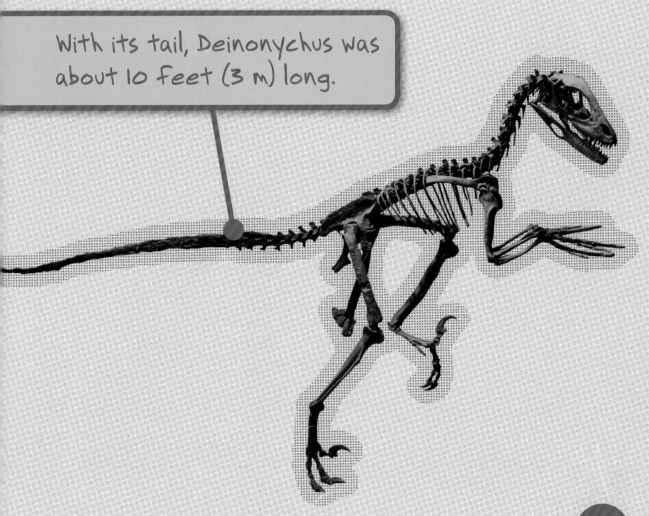

With its tail, Deinonychus was about 10 feet (3 m) long.

Velociraptor was not as big. It was only a little taller than a turkey! It stretched about 6 feet (2 m) from head to tail.

On the Hunt

How did Velociraptor and Deinonychus find food? They followed the smell of prey. They probably hunted at night.

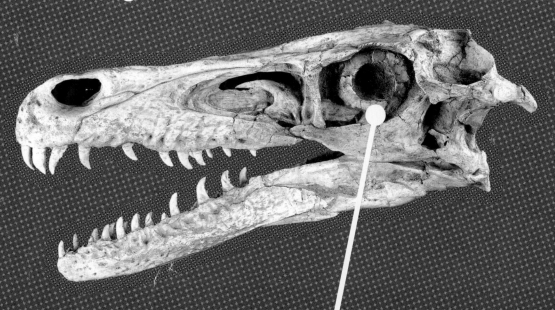

Night animals' eyes are shaped to let in light.

Some scientists think Deinonychus hunted in groups. Deinonychus packs may have attacked larger dinosaurs.

Animals that hunt together are called a pack.

Deinonychus teeth have been found with fossils of a much bigger dino. Dinosaurs sometimes lost teeth when they bit prey.

Scientists do not know if Velociraptor hunted in packs. No one has found their fossils in groups.

An artist drew this picture of Velociraptors on a hunt. But no one knows for sure how these dinos hunted.

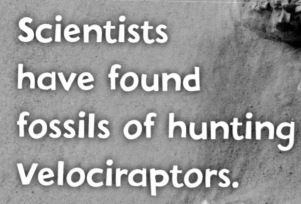

Scientists have found fossils of hunting Velociraptors.

They found a Velociraptor tangled with a Protoceratops. The two dinosaurs died in battle. Velociraptor's big claw was buried in Protoceratops's neck. Protoceratops had bitten Velociraptor's arm.

Velociraptor may also have been a scavenger. Scavengers eat dead animals that they find.

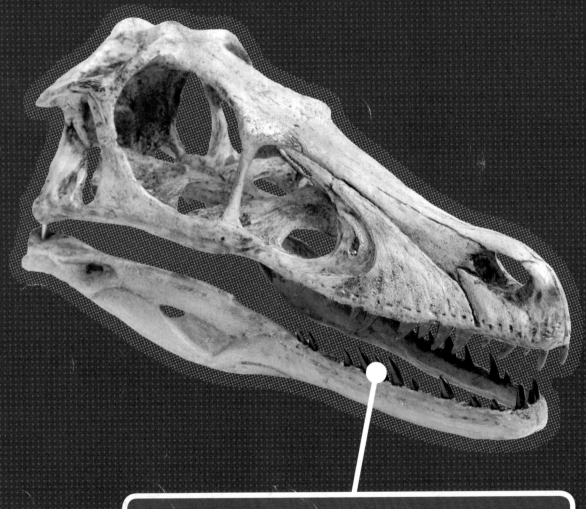

Velociraptor probably scraped meat from bones with its sharp teeth. Some Protoceratops bones have been found with tooth marks.

Feathered Dinosaurs

Velociraptor and Deinonychus were related to birds. They looked a lot like birds.

17

They had hollow bones like birds too. Hollow bones are light and strong. They help animals move fast.

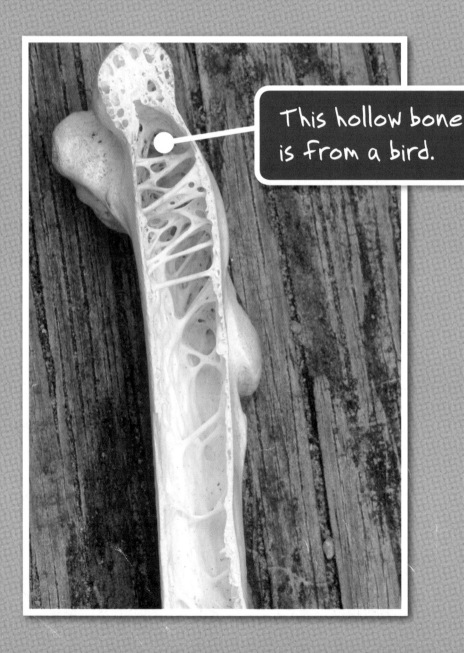

This hollow bone is from a bird.

Scientists found tiny bumps on Velociraptor's arm bones. The bumps show where feathers were attached. They prove that Velociraptor had feathers.

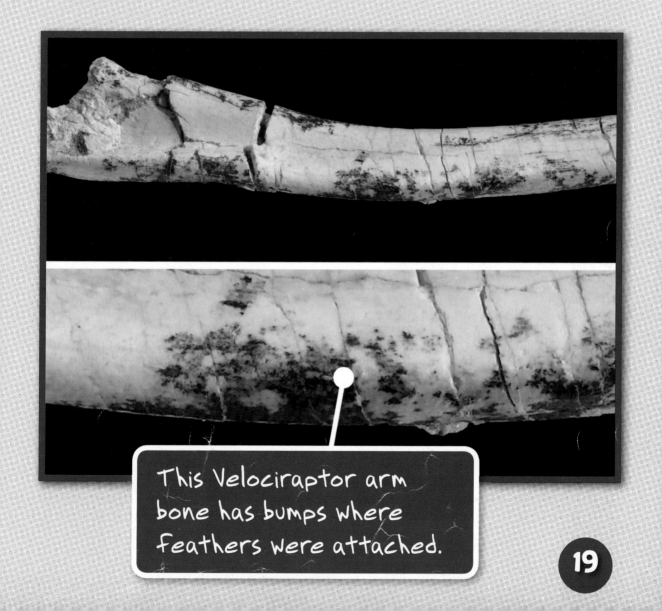

This Velociraptor arm bone has bumps where feathers were attached.

No fossils show that Deinonychus had feathers. But scientists think it did. Deinonychus probably stood on its struggling prey. It may have flapped feathered arms for balance.

Feathers probably helped these animals stay warm. The dinos may have hidden food under their feathers to keep other animals from stealing it. Their feathers may have helped them attract mates.

An artist moves a model of Deinonychus that he created.

These dinos could also have used feathered arms to warm their eggs. A Deinonychus skeleton was found with an egg.

This oviraptor uses its feathers to keep its eggs warm.

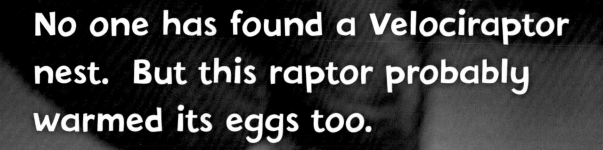

No one has found a Velociraptor nest. But this raptor probably warmed its eggs too.

These Velociraptor eggs became fossils over time.

Long Ago and Far Away

Deinonychus lived millions of years before Velociraptor. Deinonychus lived 115 to 108 million years ago.

Velociraptor fossils are not as old. This dinosaur lived **75** to **71** million years ago.

Deinonychus could not have hunted this Velociraptor.

Deinonychus roamed near rivers and swamps. People have dug up its bones in the western United States.

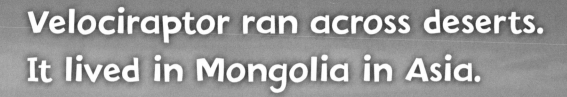

Velociraptor ran across deserts.
It lived in Mongolia in Asia.

Velociraptor fossils have
been found in this area
of the Gobi Desert.

Dino Diagrams

Can you tell these dinosaurs apart?

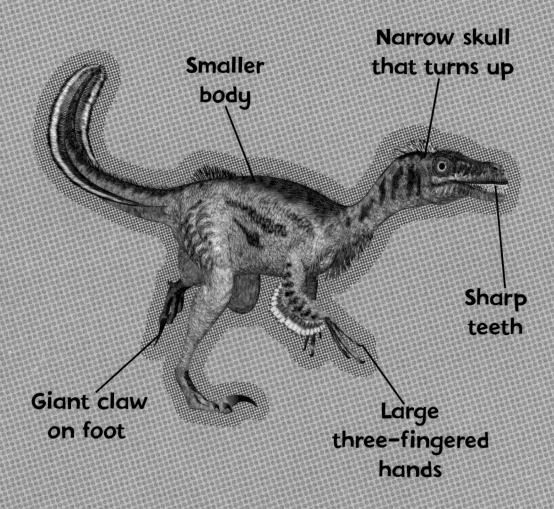

Smaller body

Narrow skull that turns up

Sharp teeth

Giant claw on foot

Large three-fingered hands

Velociraptor

Deinonychus

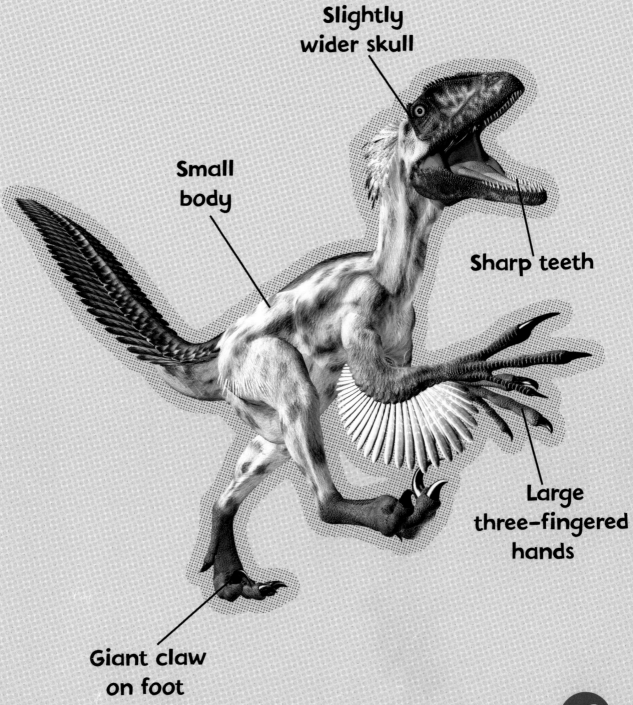

Slightly wider skull

Sharp teeth

Small body

Large three-fingered hands

Giant claw on foot

29

Glossary

fossil: the remains of a living thing from a long time ago

hollow: having an empty space inside

pack: a group of animals that runs and hunts together

predator: an animal that hunts other animals

prey: an animal that is hunted for food

raptor: a group of hunting dinosaurs that walked on two legs; had large, three-fingered hands; and had a large, curved claw on each foot

scavenger: an animal that feeds on dead matter

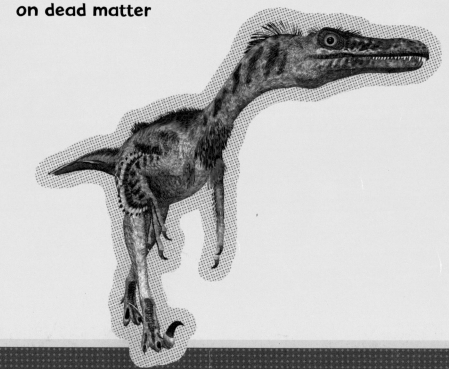

Further Reading

Brecke, Nicole, and Patricia M. Stockland. *Dinosaurs and Other Prehistoric Creatures You Can Draw.* Minneapolis: Millbrook Press, 2010.

Deinonychus Facts for Kids
http://www.sciencekids.co.nz/sciencefacts/dinosaurs/deinonychus.html

Flesh Out a Fossil
http://www.amnh.org/explore/curriculum-collections/dinosaurs-ancient-fossils-new-discoveries/flesh-out-a-fossil

Henry, Michel. *Raptor: The Life of a Young Deinonychus.* New York: Abrams Books for Young Readers, 2007.

Mara, Wil. *Velociraptor.* New York: Children's Press, 2012.

West, David. *Velociraptor and Other Raptors and Small Carnivores.* New York: Gareth Stevens Publishing, 2011.

LERNER *e* SOURCE™

Expand learning beyond the printed book. Download free, complementary educational resources for this book from our website, www.lerneresource.com.

Index

Photo Acknowledgments

The images in this book are used with the permission of: © Sergey Krasovskiy/Stocktrek Images/Getty Images, p. 1 (top); © Emily Willoughby/Stocktrek Images/CORBIS, pp. 1 (bottom), 20, 24; © Ralf Kraft/Dreamstime.com, p. 2; © MIRO3D/Bigstock.com, p. 4; © Chris Butler/Science Source, p. 5; © imagebroker.net/SuperStock, p. 6; © Louie Psihoyos/CORBIS, pp. 7, 15, 25; Didier Descouens (CC-BY-SA-3.0), p. 8; AStrangerintheAlps/Wikimedia Commons, p. 9; © Kayte Deioma/ZUMA Press/CORBIS, p. 10; © Francois Gohier/Gaston Design/Science Source, p. 11; © Laurie O'Keefe/Science Source, p. 12; © Dorling Kindersley/Getty Images, p. 13; © Mark Stevenson/Stocktrek Images/CORBIS, p. 14; © iStockphoto.com/Jeff Chiasson, p. 16; © iStockphoto.com/Mike Rodriguez, p. 17; © Gilbert S. Grant/Science Source, p. 18; AP Photo/American Museum of Natural History, Mick Ellison, p. 19; © ZUMA Press, Inc./Alamy, p. 21; © Julius T. Csotonyi/Science Source, p. 22; © wonderlandstock/Alamy, p. 23; © Stocktrek Images/SuperStock, p. 26; © Kaehler, Wolfgang/SuperStock, p. 27; © Linda Bucklin/Dreamstime.com, p. 28; © Mr1805/Dreamstime.com, pp. 29, 30.

Front Cover: © Mr1805/Dreamstime.com (both).

Main body text set in Johann Light 30/36.